MISSISSIPPI RIVER

MISSISSIPPI
River

Photographs by Jerry Stebbins

Text by Barbara Cameron

ST. MARTIN'S PRESS

New York

ALSO BY JERRY STEBBINS
(with text by Greg Breining)

Boundary Waters

Front-matter photographs

First half-title page. Towboat and barge heading upriver near Prescott, Wisconsin
Full-title page. Sunset on the lower Mississippi
Copyright page. Cajun craftsman, Cocodri, Louisiana
Opposite copyright page. Delta Queen paddlewheel
Second half-title. Evening on the river, near Ft. Snelling in Minnesota

Design by Jerry Stebbins and Claire Counihan

Library of Congress Cataloging-in-Publication Data
Stebbins, Jerry.
    Mississippi River.
      1. Mississippi River—Description and travel—Views. 2. Mississippi River Valley—Description and travel—Views.   I. Cameron, Barbara, 1947-
II. Title.
F355.S74   1987   977   87-4726
ISBN 0-312-00922-4

First Edition
10 9 8 7 6 5 4 3 2 1

Acknowledgment is made to the following sources, from which various short passages have been excerpted:

Recollections of the Last Ten Years in the Valley of the Mississippi, Timothy Flint, ed. George R. Brooks (Carbondale: Southern Illinois University Press, 1968), copyright © 1968 by Southern Illinois University Press. (Flint was originally published by Cummings, Hilliard, and Company in Boston, 1826.)
The Valley of the Mississippi Illustrated, Henry Lewis, ed. Bertha L. Heilbron (St. Paul: Minnesota Historical Society, 1967), copyright © 1967 by Minnesota Historical Society. (Lewis was originally published in German by Arnz and Company of Düsseldorf, 1854.)
Life on the Mississippi, Mark Twain (New York: Airmont Publishing Company, Inc., 1965 paperback edition), copyright © 1965 by Airmont Publishing Company, Inc. (Twain was originally published in 1883.)
Father Louis Hennepin's Description of Louisiana, trans. Marion E. Cross (University of Minnesota Press, 1938), copyright © 1938 by University of Minnesota.
The Wild Palms, William Faulkner (New York: Random House, Inc., 1939), copyright © 1939 by William Faulkner.
Delta Wedding, Eudora Welty (New York: Harcourt Brace Jovanovich, 1979), copyright © 1945 by Eudora Welty.
Listening Point, Sigurd F. Olson (New York: Alfred A. Knopf, 1982), copyright © 1958 by Sigurd F. Olson.
Schoolcraft's Expedition to Lake Itasca, ed. Philip P. Mason (East Lansing: Michigan State University Press, 1958), copyright © 1958 by Michigan State University Press.
Land of the Long Horizons, ed. Walter Havighurst (New York: Coward-McCann, Inc., 1960), copyright © 1960 by Walter Havighurst.
River World, Virginia S. Eifert (New York: Dodd, Mead & Company, 1959), copyright © 1959 by Virginia S. Eifert.
The Last of the Middle West, J. R. Humphreys (Garden City, New York: Doubleday and Company, Inc., 1966), copyright © 1962 by J. R. Humphreys.
Selections from "Minnesota History," A Fiftieth Anniversary Anthology, eds. Rhoda R. Gilman and June Drenning Holmquist (St. Paul: Minnesota Historical Society, 1965), copyright © 1965 by Minnesota Historical Society.
Explorers of the Mississippi, Timothy Severin (New York: Alfred A. Knopf, 1968), copyright © 1967 by Timothy Severin.
Before Mark Twain: A Sampler of Old, Old Times on the Mississippi, ed. John Francis McDermott (Carbondale: Southern Illinois University Press, 1968), copyright © 1968 by Southern Illinois University Press.
The Journals of Joseph N. Nicollet, ed. Martha Coleman Bray (St. Paul: Minnesota Historical Society, 1970), copyright © 1970 by Minnesota Historical Society.
Old Glory, An American Voyage, Jonathan Raban (New York: Simon and Schuster, 1981), copyright © 1981 by Jonathan Raban.
Mighty Mississippi, Marquis W. Childs (New Haven and New York: Ticknor & Fields, 1982), copyright © 1982 by Marquis W. Childs.

I would like to thank the following people for their assistance in making this book a reality: Malcomb Magruder and Norton Stillman, for the idea; Bruce Morgan and Al Gedoi of the Louisiana Department of Tourism; Captains Brough, Foley, and Hillman of the Delta Queen Steamboat Company; Dan Marrone; Swamp Annie; Anne Harmon; Gary Young; G_2; and Barbara Anderson.

This book is dedicated to my wife, Barb, and to my family: Dick, Micky, Cathy, Joel, Jeff, Richard, and Jennifer.

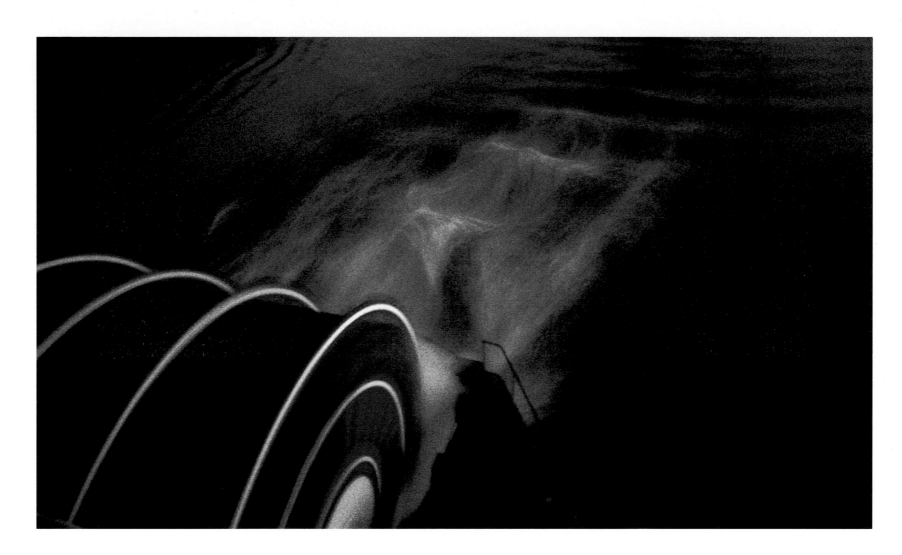

CONTENTS

INTRODUCTION

MISSISSIPPI. The sounds come from an Algonquian language of long ago, yet the syllables are music, familiar on any tongue. They name the river of our imagination, so celebrated by Mark Twain: "the great Mississippi, the majestic, the magnificent Mississippi, rolling its mile-wide tide along, shining in the sun."

No other river claims our attention in quite the same way. The Mississippi's watershed takes in one and a quarter million square miles, nearly half the continental United States. Of all the world's rivers, only the Amazon and Congo basins are greater. At approximately 2,350 miles, the Mississippi rates little more than half the measure of the Nile, the longest river, but her own longest tributary, the Missouri, makes the Mississippi system over five thousand miles long—by far the largest river system on earth. Because the Mississippi is a meandering river, given to frequent course corrections by

Above. Sunrise, south of Hannibal, Missouri

cutoffs and channel changes, her actual length is always in flux.

The Mississippi accepts tribute from 250 streams. Water and sediment of thirty-one states and two Canadian provinces are borne from as far west as Montana and Wyoming, from as far east as New York and North Carolina. The river borders ten states, flowing through the country's heartland from its sources in northern Minnesota to its delta in Louisiana.

The great Mississippi releases 2,300,000 cubic feet of water per second into the Gulf of Mexico. Some 400 million cubic yards of mud, sand, and gravel are carried seaward each year. That translates into about two million tons of sediment reaching the delta every day.

It would be difficult to ignore the Mississippi River. Its economic immediacy touches the lives of everyone who lives in a river town, whether through employment on a barge loading grain in the twin cities of St. Paul and Minneapolis or promoting tourism in Hannibal, Missouri. The Mississippi Valley accounts for about three-quarters of the country's gross national product in agriculture, commerce, and industry.

The vital pulse of the Mississippi's physical presence is an underlay to the lives of the millions who live in the Mississippi Valley. More than any other river, this is a great and unifying landform. It connects independent loggers working the northern Minnesota woods to corn farmers in Iowa and Illinois, the cotton hands toiling behind the levees in Arkansas and Mississippi to self-reliant Cajuns netting crawdaddies in delta backwaters.

The Mississippi affects people deeply, intimately. Personal journals kept by the early explorers give us a notion of the immensity of the Mississippi— its physical beauty and grandeur, its incredible breadth at flood stage. The Mississippi of the early days must have given pause to the human spirit. It was a riverscape so wild, so untouched, so entire unto itself, that the passage of a mere human being might hardly be noticed.

In many ways it is still the same for us, today. We've all heard stories about this river, probably since childhood. It remains a metaphor of wonder and adventure, incredibly powerful. It is the archetypal river of the American imagination, for the Mississippi has had everything to do with the growth of the nation, the formation of her people. It has become part of our psyche, ever present, ever moving, ever changing. The Mississippi flows through our lives in much the way memory does—at times murky, then clearing. Rising and falling, it may shift direction. Like dream, it can inspire both comfort and fear.

The Mississippi is a river born in legend, the essence of dream. The French, first Europeans to hear tell of the "great river" from the northern Indians in the early sixteenth century, were searching for the elusive passage to China. They assumed this river would be their key to the Orient.

It wasn't until 1541 that the first white man happened upon the Mississippi River—by accident. This was a Spaniard, also looking for legendary wealth, but a muddy river was no part of his plan. All he wanted was to cross its dangerous width and get on with his exploration.

Remarkably, 132 years would elapse before another European dipped paddle in the Mississippi River, and nearly three centuries would pass before its headwaters were correctly located. By that time, the fabulous waterway down the middle of the continent was beginning to be recognized for what it really was: the lifestream of the richest river valley on earth.

Only one of the early European explorers, La Salle, had understood what a powerful social and political reality this extraordinary river represented. He was well ahead of his time in trying to unite an empire north/south along the axis of the Mississippi River; indeed, he claimed the entire territory for France in 1682. He foresaw its possibilities for trade and transportation, agriculture and defense, but it remained for Americans of the nineteenth century to begin to transform that vision into their own reality.

Mississippi lands were moving from French and Spanish into American hands in the late eighteenth century. With President Jefferson's Louisiana Purchase in 1803, the entire Mississippi River Valley was opened to Ameri-can settlers. They came in their thousands, family by family. On foot across the Appalachians, by flatboat and keelboat down the broad Ohio, and—later —by rail, immigrants came to meet the Mississippi and their future in the West. Up the great river they pushed, the settlers often stopping in places that bore no name. Some of these landings became major riverports of their day, and furs and hides, corn, wheat, and flour, lead and timber made their way downriver to markets in St. Louis and New Orleans.

The river presented a magnificent pageant of life to nineteenth-century immigrants and travelers, but it was a setting so awesome that artists like Henry Lewis thought of it as "a *solitude,* vast and lonely." The big river inspired big art: painted panoramas of the riverscape up to three miles long, unrolling from spools of canvas twelve feet high. Spellbound audiences on the East Coast and around the world marveled at the spectacle before them, and many came to see the river for themselves.

In the mid-nineteenth century, steamboats forged up and down the river, hauling cargo and passengers. This was the era made famous by Mark Twain, the golden time before railroads effectively displaced riverboats. For Twain—and many of his readers—this technological change in the direction of progress was almost a loss of innocence. The river was still there, but we seemed no longer to hear her voice.

The great river, though, has always spoken to the mysterious urgings of birds; the Mississippi flyway is the longest and most heavily traveled in North America. Swans and Canada geese, nighthawks, loons, and wood ducks, vireos, finches, scarlet tanagers, and swallows . . . they all follow the map of the Mississippi.

The Mississippi provides an amazing diversity of habitat for plants and animals. But it does something else, too. Just as the Mississippi weaves the colorful threads of creation into a living fabric, so too does she entwine human lives in the texture of her garment. The river draws the natural world together into one piece, and we become a part of that threading together of the continuity of life.

The Mississippi River rolls on, a tremendous gathering of waters, of lives, through the seasons of creation, in an unending cycle of renewal.

Even as the current bears us along this most public of watercourses, the river also calls to private places in our personal memories. The images in this book are one man's vision of the ever-changing Mississippi; the text is intended to complement that sense of the personal within the public. We hope the collection is a tribute to the reality of the Mississippi, to her extraordinary beauty and terror. As Mark Twain so truly said, "It is not a commonplace river, but on the contrary is in all ways remarkable."

Barbara Cameron
Deer River, Minnesota
1987

MISSISSIPPI
RIVER

MISSISSIPPI
Headwaters

THE headwaters is a place of beginnings. *Mississippi* comes from the Algonquian for "great river," but here, trickling over stones at its narrow outlet from Lake Itasca, the Father of Waters is but a baby, mere inches deep, and very quiet. Step into these sandy shallows on a summer's morning, nudge the pebbles in that tiny, crystalline stream, and consider how a big idea begins.

Breathe deeply the redolent pitch of virgin pine, centuries old. Recall the busy timber years after 1855, when the Ojibway Indians ceded the watershed area to the government. Choppers and sawyers cut into the forests all winter. Countless horse-drawn sleighs hauled hundred-ton loads to the riverbank. When streams swelled with meltwater in spring, many lumberjacks became "river pigs," driving their logs from the landings to the mills. Then, within the space of a man's lifetime, the boom was over, the big pines gone.

To sense the mystery of this northern region, the boreal spirit of the place, stand quietly at the headwaters and listen to the night. The bedrock deep beneath your feet was present even as the planet was being formed. In air so clear, the stars seem to crackle. Inevitably your eye seeks the North Star. Direction must be taken, your place confirmed.

Boreal. The very word suggests north winds, extreme cold. And cold, not warmth, is the key to this place.

Four times in the last million years the northern hemisphere wore a mantle of blue ice more than a mile thick. Four times these great ice fields melted back, reshaping the face of the earth, filling enormous lakes and rivers with glacial meltwaters. Ten thousand years ago, during the end of the last ice age, the Mississippi River headwaters began to take form. Man was already here during that harsh boreal winter, hunting the musk ox and mastodon, long-horn bison and giant beaver.

Later he would know copper, the gathering of wild rice, and the coming of the white man. Ojibway prophecy anticipated all these things. Somewhere in the telling,

Left. Stepping stones at the Mississippi headwaters

Above. Northern sky at night over the headwaters

11

recorded time merged with mythic time. The Ojibway culture hero of sacred memory, Nanabozho, crossed the Great River on his travels before his people began their own westward migration toward the Mississippi during historical times. On his journey he learned that the cup of life is water.

This river is still the cup of life for much of a continent. The Mississippi embraces thirty-one states and two Canadian provinces within its drainage basin. About a third of all the rainwater falling on the continental United States is carried directly to the sea; the Mississippi alone gathers forty percent of that run-off. Rising from spruce bogs in the Minnesota north woods, then draining the nation's heartland between the Rockies and the Appalachians, the Mississippi lifts two million tons of sediment from one and a quarter million square miles of land every day—and carries it off, along the borders of ten states, to the Gulf of Mexico.

It's only six or seven steps across the stones at Lake Itasca. Given this river's reputation, you might well be surprised at such modest beginnings. Nevertheless, even here, looking downstream a hundred feet, you can see what's happening . . . twigs catching crossways on each other, miniature sandbars shifting around on the bottom, water making eddies around rocks.

The Great River is getting ready.

Left. "It must be one of the very few major rivers in the world which develops meander loops within walking distance of its source."
—Timothy Severin,
Explorers of the Mississippi, 1968

Preceding pages. Tamarack trees at Lake Itasca

Above. The Mississippi River leaving Lake Itasca

Right. The Mississippi begins as an unspoiled, unpeopled wilderness stream heading north to Bemidji.

YOU are in Indian country. Bemidji, Winnibigoshish, Leech Lake, Mud Lake, Vermilion, Pokegama, Deer River. An Ojibway Indian, Oza Windib, guided Schoolcraft's expedition to the lake his people knew as Moskos. Three hours after reaching the headwaters and renaming the lake Itasca, Schoolcraft left, following the emergent Mississippi River. "We soon felt . . . a current, and began to glide, with velocity, down a clear stream with a sandy and pebbly bottom, strewed with shells and overhung by foliage."

Four years later Joseph Nicollet made extensive maps of the Mississippi headwaters area. He detailed an important bit of information about the heights of land in northern Minnesota. The region is a three-way watershed, such that drainage can be north through the Red River to Hudson Bay, east to Lake Superior and the Atlantic, or south to the Gulf of Mexico.

Nicollet was unusual in his appreciation of the vitality of the people living in this wild region. But he was also a man of another world, a European who recognized that change must inevitably result from his work along the river. That uniquely American sense of a manifest destiny was not yet national doctrine, but we can hear it coming in Nicollet's journal. He speaks of wanting to find the route "that would contribute the most to the development of trade and the arrival of the civilization that will soon be knocking on the door of these solitudes."

That word so peculiar to the nineteenth century—solitudes—still defines much of our sense of the river and her landscape as we pass from Lake Itasca. Beautiful, but not really hospitable. It is wilderness. It does not require our presence. Instead, we sense a serene detachment about being here, on this river.

It is easy to get lost, even to lose the river in the headwaters area. It may seem that the river herself doesn't know where she is going. For sixty miles it flows north; then it heads east another 120 miles toward Lake Superior. After Grand Rapids it is decidedly flowing toward the Gulf.

Until Bemidji, the river is a wilderness stream. Except for the humming of diaphanous clouds of insects during the warm season, it is quiet. In the summer, mosquitoes and biting flies drive crazed whitetails into the water to seek relief. Black bears and even an occasional moose range these marshes and conifer forests. Beavers alter the tributary streams to their own purposes. Muskrats you'll see, and redwings flagging the cattails, but not many people along this stretch.

After Bemidji, the Mississippi is a river-lake chain. By 1890 the federal government had completed four major regulatory dams on headwater lakes to create a system of controlled reservoirs for the benefit of industry downstream.

The river flows on through Cass Lake to give you a charming surprise, like a Chinese puzzle: in the middle of the lake is Star Island, and from the island's heart shines tiny Lake Windigo, named for the Indian spirit of mischief. Now we approach an area of thick grasses and sedges and reeds in the vicinity of Lake Winnibigoshish.

Winnibigoshish ("miserable-wretched-dirty-water") is some seventeen by fifteen miles long; it seems an endless expanse. A storm quickly roils up mud and sand from the bottom. Lake Winni is fairly shallow, but a wind renders the open water dangerously choppy. This sudden evidence of the power of the Nebenawbaig, the water spirits, reminds you this is no ordinary lake; Winnibigoshish is part of the ever-changing face of the Mississippi River.

THE prehistoric Indian ancestors moving along these northern courses of the Mississippi headwaters region when the last glacial ice receded were subsistence foragers. They must have carried a complicated survival map in their heads: knowledge of the terrain, the know-how to craft appropriate tools and weapons, familiarity with the migration patterns of game animals and the seasonal cycles of wild plants.

As the northern climate continued to change, pine forests gradually replaced the savanna. By 800 A.D., woodland peoples had learned to preserve and store the wild rice they harvested. Populations grew and semipermanent villages were established as small bands traveled between the sugar bush and the ricing camps.

The Ojibway consider manomin, or wild rice, a sacred gift, freely offered them in the broad shallows of headwater lakes. Limp young blades of green lie on the water's surface in late spring, and then, during the August rice moon, the stalks stand eight feet tall. At summer's end the mature rice is harvested by pairs of ricers, one poling the canoe, the other beating the heavy rice heads into the bottom of the boat.

The French *coureurs des bois* and the missionary priests who penetrated the wilderness in the seventeenth century by way of Hudson Bay and the Great Lakes learned to eat wild rice, and they soon adopted the northern Indians' mode of navigation: the birch bark canoe. Here was a technology of grace, ideally and specifically suited to its environment. Light enough for one person to portage, a small bark canoe could be maneuvered with just one paddle. It floated like a leaf on the water, barely skimming the surface of lakes and streams, darting over small rapids. It slipped through marshes as easily as a northern pike glided through the weeds below.

Indians peeled off the aromatic cinnamon-brown bark in broad sheets from the upper portion of the trees when the sap was rising in springtime. These rolls of bark were then flexed over the white cedar ribs of the canoe and stitched together using the pliant roots of black spruce. Caulking the holes with a gum made of boiled spruce resin ensured a watertight craft. Porcupine quillwork added a distinctive touch of beauty.

Two centuries after Europeans first entered the northern forests, the artist Henry Lewis was impressed by the natural bounty enjoyed by northern Indians, especially the Ojibway, or Chippewa:

> Among all the Indian tribes, the Chippewa who live near the sources of the Mississippi seem to be most favored by nature. They have fish of all kinds, wild rice, maple sugar and game in abundance; the climate is particularly well suited to . . . corn, wheat, barley . . . and potatoes . . . Hunting provides . . . bear, deer, elk, wolves, foxes, wolverines, otter, polecats, raccoons, marten, weasels, beaver . . . , and one may assume that this is . . . where the finer sorts of pelts are to be found.

He also remarked that even in the midst of plenty, Chippewa parents encouraged fasting so their children would "more easily endure the periods of hunger . . . that become more frequent as the giant arm of civilization pushes back the Indians, decreasing the amount of game and other natural products."

Above. The Pine River, an excellent canoe stream, joins the Mississippi in the Crow Wing State Forest above Brainerd.

Right. An Ojibway boy spears for suckers near the Winnibigoshish Dam, Minnesota. "The day he can venture alone . . . from the village, he hunts. . . . From this time onward the child always remains active . . . makes his own bows, spears . . ."
—Joseph Nicollet, *Journal,* 1836

LOONS. Their primordial, haunting voices beckon to us across mythic time.

In one version of the Ojibway creation story, floodwaters covered the earth, and man was stranded on a floating log, unable to swim to the bottom. Loon was the first earthdiver among the animals. He sacrificed himself in the effort to collect a piece of precious soil for earth's re-creation.

Northern dwellers still prize the loon, for its presence is a measure of the vitality of woodland waters, a tangible confirmation of the wilderness values inherent in their way of life.

Listen with Sigurd Olson:

Above came a swift whisper of wings, and as the loons saw us they called wildly in alarm, increased the speed of their flight, and took their laughing with them into the gathering dusk. . . . The shores echoed and re-echoed until they seemed to throb with the music. This was . . . the sound that more than any other typifies the rocks and waters and forests of the wilderness.

That thrilling, mysterious voice calls to us from the depths of fossil time—eighty million years of loons in wilderness waters. Their descendants continue to breed in these headwaters, then follow the Mississippi flyway to the Gulf Coast. Predators will get 75 percent of loon chicks, but people are the real stress on the species. Human notions of development generally mean loon habitat destruction, whether through clearing a shoreline of weeds or producing acid rain.

Loons will share these waters with us, but only if their environment can remain protected and relatively undisturbed.

Left. The common loon does not frequent small lakes; it requires up to one-quarter mile of water runway to get airborne.

MISSISSIPPI
Upper River

THE upper Mississippi is stage to an ever-flowing pageant of life. It is a kaleidoscope of shifting images, illusory and ambiguous, filled with possibility and open to interpretation. As the scene changes, your fancy takes over: the slough fisherman yonder dissolves into a seventeenth-century explorer-priest. And what blessing does he imagine on such a morning, on such a river?

Mist rises over vast reaches of the upper Mississippi backwaters; cattails and water lilies come into view, yellow lotus delights the eye. Here is life abundant, the wilderness promise fulfilled. Waterfowl and wading birds, muskrat and beaver, catfish and walleye share this bottomland with farmers, fishermen, and all manner of river traffic and travelers.

French mapmakers were the first to chart the upper river's course. Since the early seventeenth century they had been searching for the fabled water route to China. In 1673, Joliet and Marquette demonstrated the futility of that effort when they followed the Mississippi for a thousand miles below the Wisconsin River and concluded that the great river flowed into the Gulf of Mexico and not to the Pacific and beyond. They were the first white men to experience the infinite solitude of the upper river, its dense forests, high bluffs, open prairies. The magnificence of the Mississippi above the Wisconsin's mouth was documented by another Frenchman, Father Hennepin, who christened the falls at St. Anthony.

The falls, located just above the twin cities of Minneapolis and St. Paul, divide the upper Mississippi from the headwaters, and they are the most significant geological formation on the Mississippi. They determined much of the economic life of the river, too, for without the falls there would have been no lumber or flour milling industries at the head of navigation.

Left. Beef Slough, an upper Mississippi fishing spot

Above. Towboat negotiating the bends and islands of the upper Mississippi

After the Louisiana Purchase put the entire Mississippi Valley into American hands in 1803, the new owners were interested to know more about the lay of the land—and their river. The upper Mississippi captured the frontier imagination. Land-hungry farmers, unemployed miners, shopkeepers and tradespeople, actors and gamblers—working folk of every description packed their belongings and made their way to the river. On the crowded riverboats religious zealots rubbed shoulders with land speculators; everyone was looking for a new life.

As people settled upriver, the fruits of their industry were shipped downriver. Timothy Flint noted "boats loaded with corn in bulk, and in the ear. Others are loaded with pork in bulk. Others with barrels of apples and potatoes . . . furniture, tools, domestic and agricultural implements."

The steamboats' energetic part in the country's growth would decline after 1856, when the first railroad bridge to span the Mississippi joined Davenport, Iowa, and Rock Island, Illinois.

The upper Mississippi continues to be a bustling watercourse, a working river in a setting of unique natural beauty. The seasons control the shipping schedules here; farmers gather the harvest while the sun shines, and barges move before winter's ice locks them out for several months. Such necessity makes for a pragmatic vitality among people on the upper river.

Left. St. Anthony Falls today, boxed up by the lock and dam, hemmed in by the bridge and freeway system

Left. More bridges span the Mississippi in St. Paul and Minneapolis than at any other city on the river.

Right. Tons of low-sulphur coal move through St. Paul from western mines.

T the confluence of the Mississippi and Minnesota rivers was a precipitous bluff commanding a fine view of the future—so thought Lieutenant Zebulon Pike. He was much pleased with himself for the handsome land purchases he negotiated with the Sioux for half a barrel of whiskey in 1805. One of those parcels was the site of the future Fort St. Anthony (Fort Snelling).

Three hundred soldiers laboriously poled their keelboats up the Mississippi in 1819 to begin construction of the frontier's most remote military outpost. That first winter they suffered the malignant scurvy and other discomforts of wilderness life. After passing to Colonel Snelling's command the following year, though, the little fort would thrive. The soldiers' job was to protect the American fur trade against incursion from the British and to control the Indians.

The fort began operating successful grist and saw mills, and access to the Falls of St. Anthony became very desirable. Security provided by the military presence drew settlers and business strategists to this part of the upper river wilderness, and St. Anthony, St. Paul, and Minneapolis established themselves on the Mississippi. Minneapolis became a milling giant, and St. Paul became the commercial center at the head of navigation on the Mississippi.

After the *Virginia,* first steamboat to ply the waters of the upper Mississippi, reached the falls in 1823, the fort itself became a fashionable stop along the upper Mississippi touring route. Thus did the men of Fort Snelling enjoy an unexpected social life on the frontier.

Above. The Round Tower at Fort Snelling is a storied place. Dred Scott was married here in 1837; young Count Zeppelin conducted balloon experiments from the tower after the Civil War.

Left. The Levee neighborhood, St. Paul

Above. ". . . great volumes of the blackest
smoke are rolling and tumbling out of the
chimneys—a husbanded grandeur created with
a bit of pitch pine just before arriving at a
town . . ."
   —MARK TWAIN, *Life on the Mississippi,* 1883

Preceding pages. St. Paul at sunset from
Mounds Park, overlooking the river.

Above. Captain Foley is the oldest pilot on the Mississippi. Twain said a pilot "was the only unfettered and entirely independent human being that lived in the earth. . . . The moment that the boat was under way in the river, she was under the sole and unquestioned control of the pilot."

Above. Separation of a tow to be accommodated in a lock on the upper river. Fifteen barges is the maximum.

Right. A modern deckhand

BARGES have been the preeminent traffic on the Mississippi River since World War I. They have tremendous carrying capacity; a single barge can hold over a million gallons of oil, or 85,000 bushels of grain. Several barges strung together in a tow make a moving platform over a thousand feet long, larger than an ocean liner.

The Army Corps of Engineers maintains a complex system of locks and dams to accommodate the barge traffic, twenty-nine installations between St. Louis and St. Anthony Falls. Until locks were built to "stair-step" vessels over changes in the river's elevation, such as rapids and waterfalls, St. Paul was as far as a barge could go unaided.

The lock at Upper St. Anthony Falls lifts boats and barges 49.2 feet—higher than any other single lock on the Mississippi, or even on the Panama Canal. A very efficient operation, it requires but eight minutes to fill or empty the chamber.

Modern locks and dams make it possible for huge quantities of fuel and foodstuffs to move throughout mid-America. The army engineers on the dredge *Thompson* keep a nine-foot-deep commercial navigation channel open between St. Paul and St. Louis.

Despite these navigational control efforts along the upper river, big barge tows today encounter many of the same difficulties their nineteenth-century forerunners did. Huge, unwieldy timber rafts, pushed by steamboat, could cover up to two acres of water, and they had to cross Lake Pepin on their way to market in St. Louis. The river pilots found this "wide-place-in-the-river" to be as treacherous as it was lovely, subject to upstream winds and violent storms. The river can still upend a barge as easily as a little pleasure craft, or snatch a barge from its tow and send it careening into another vessel, or into shore. A barge run amok can easily run into the millions of dollars in damages.

Barge damage to shorelines is one of the continuing complaints of residents in upper river communities. The irony is perhaps more obvious in the smaller towns like Reads Landing or Fountain City, towns that once handled tremendous volumes of river traffic. The heavy barges no longer stop; there's not enough business. The barges just lock through on their way to more lucrative landings.

OUNTAIN CITY, Wisconsin, named for the free-flowing springs in its bluffs, is an intimate river community, the kind of town that comes right down to the bank to greet you, much as it did one hundred years ago. An independent frontiersman made the first squatter's claim in 1839; but he was the sort of fellow to whom solitude was a necessity, civilization a burden. After other white men came to stay, Mr. Holmes felt crowded and chose to cross the river and go further west.

Holmes Landing became Fountain City, and the industrious Swiss, German, and Polish settlers traded with the Indians, sold cordwood to the steamboatmen going to Fort Snelling, and supplied the river travelers with all manner of goods.

People who live on the upper Mississippi feel a particular closeness to their river. Its banks are well defined, and while there will be seasons of high and low water, the river itself is mainly a positive presence in peoples' lives. They respond to its magic. The water is still clean enough to swim in, and the richness of aquatic wildlife enhances the vividness of their lives.

The upper river sustains heavy recreational use, especially the wilderness refuge encompassing some 200,000 acres along both banks from Lake Pepin downstream to Rock Island, Illinois. Many small towns on the river, like Fountain City, have already seen their heyday in lumber, steamboat supply, or commercial fishing. Now the Mississippi is important to them for its aesthetic and entertainment values. The river and its wetlands and backwaters are prime territories for boating and canoeing, waterfowling, hunting, and sportfishing.

Above. The common egret has made a comeback in backwater rookeries of the Upper Mississippi River Wildlife and Fish Refuge. Created by Congress in 1924, this unique river wilderness area crosses four states and is open to public use.

Right. Fountain City, Wisconsin

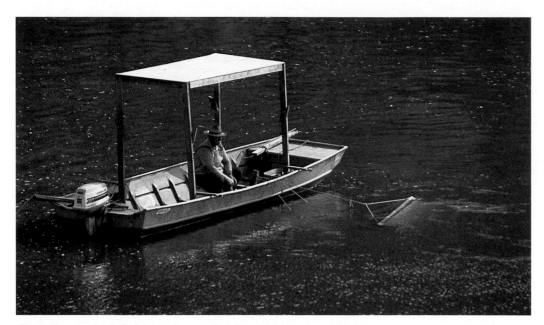

Preceding pages. A freight train crossing the river between Wisconsin, near Perrot State Park, and Winona, Minnesota

Above. Freshwater clams need ten years to reach minimal commercial size. They used to live twenty to forty years or more, but with overfishing and habitat destruction, it's hard to find an old clam these days.

Right. Butch Enge with buffalofish, Genoa, Wisconsin

EW of us will ever experience the singularity of Mississippi aquatic life Father Marquette observed from his canoe in 1673:

> From time to time we came upon monstrous Fish, one of which struck our Canoe with such violence that I Thought it was a great tree, about to break the Canoe to pieces. . . . When we cast our nets into the water we caught Sturgeon, and a very extraordinary Kind of fish. It resembles the trout, with This difference, that its mouth is larger. Near its nose which is smaller, as are also the eyes—is a large Bone shaped like a woman's busk, three fingers wide and a Cubit Long, at the end of which is a disk as Wide as one's hand.

Their catch was a paddlefish, a creature distantly related to prehistoric sharks. It has no scales, and a cartilaginous rather than a bony skeleton. It used to reach the size and weight of a man, though most paddlefish today are much smaller. It prefers to stay hidden in the deepest Mississippi waters, snooting around the bottom to filter crustaceans and insect naiads across its gill rakers.

Like the other giants of the Mississippi, the paddlefish is rare. Its only existing relative lives in the Yangtze River system of China. Despite its rarity, there is new commercial interest in the paddlefish: for caviar. It is the misfortune of this species to produce roe that exactly imitate those of the sevruga sturgeon, the most expensive caviar in the world.

The sturgeon is another boneless 300-million-year-old relic still surviving in the Mississippi. Eight feet long, its two-hundred-pound body is covered by bony plates that make it look impregnable, but they are no protection against its human predators. Sturgeon fishing was important during the last century, when isinglass was made from their swim bladders.

Bowfins and gars are two more ancients living in the Mississippi—fish that stayed behind in the river when others of their kind continued to evolve in salt water. They have a reputation for voracity, and some alligator gars have been caught with human remains inside.

The most valuable commercial fish taken in the Mississippi are catfish, even if they still have to overcome an undeserved reputation for unsavoriness. Buffalofish and carp thrive in warm silty waters, and they account for the greatest commercial tonnage in the river.

Left. The Mississippi exacts a prodigious tonnage of topsoil from farms along the watershed. Some Iowa counties lose thirteen tons per year, a rate three times what the farmers think is acceptable.

HE mile-square sections of planted land vary in color with crop and season as the Mississippi rolls for mile upon mile through this heartland patchwork of abundance. Stop your ears against the roar of the John Deere, then look across endless acres of ripening grain. You can appreciate the optimism of immigrant farmers making their way upriver in the early nineteenth century, drawn by the promise of fertile soil at affordable prices. Land on the exceptionally rich Muscatine prairie could be had for $1.25 an acre from the government when Henry Lewis visited in 1848.

"The soil is of the easiest culture and the most exuberant productiveness," reported a preacher who found his personal vision of the Garden on the American prairie.

The grass is thick and tall. Corn and wheat grow in the greatest perfection. . . . the soil is mellow, friable, and of an inky blackness; . . . it immediately absorbs the rain, and . . . yields generally forty bushels of wheat, and seventy of corn to the acre. The vegetable soil has a depth of forty feet, and earth thrown from the bottom of the wells is as fertile as that on the surface.

Above. Just south of Marquette, Iowa, a farmer tends to the task of baling hay.

Left. Motorboats heading upriver near
Lansing, Iowa

 IKE so many upper river communities, Lansing, Iowa, was a prosperous button town for a few short years after the turn of the century. By then her sawmills were already quiet, the gristmills closed, but the river bottom seemed to hold inexhaustible numbers of clams. Thousands of tons of shellfish were raked up yearly, and by 1912 domestic pearl buttons were a multimillion-dollar industry in the United States.

In the late thirties, as part of the federal government's plan to control Mississippi water levels, lock and dam installations were built a few miles above and below Lansing. Clam fishing continued, but the hauls were never the same after the dams.

Then came plastic, and that was virtually the end of pearl buttons. Nevertheless, there are a few clam fishers dragging their hooks over the Mississippi bottom, hoping to snag the big clam, the one with the perfect natural pearl inside.

Now the Japanese are interested in Mississippi pearls. They have discovered that pellets of iridescent nacre cut from thick-shelled Mississippi river clams make the best medium for producing cultured pearls.

The big river is still rich in small treasures.

Above. Lansing, Iowa

Right. Connecting Iowa and Wisconsin is the Blackhawk Bridge, named for the Sac chief who became a folk hero after his courageous attempt to defend his people's sacred land on the river against the U.S. Army.

Above. With blithe disregard for the big guys, a pontoon plies the river.

Above. Fishing near Marquette, Iowa

THE Mississippi comes from long ago and far away. It is part of the earth's own great circulatory system: water coming up from the aquifers moving deep beneath the earth's surface, dampening forth from the spongy ground of bogs and marshes, collecting in pools, gathering into streams, flowing into seas, evaporating into fogs and clouds, raining onto earth, seeping into the deep aquifers again. It courses with liquid that may be many thousands of years old, mixed with water that fell as rain only yesterday. Our good earth is the water planet.

Before ever it flowed, the modern Mississippi was frozen in a state of suspended animation for millenium upon millenium as glacial ice before melting into Lake Agassiz. Imagine the torrent of a million years of water coming from a lake that covered more ground than the five Great Lakes do today. When finally the ice melted, the glacial river waters scouring a canyon through the middle of the continent, it brought an abundance of life into being. That ancient lake bed itself became the rich earth of the northern prairies, where, in recent centuries, buffalo grazed in herds so large they were like another living sea moving across the land.

Preceding pages. Near the present site of Prairie du Chien, where, with Joliet in 1673, Marquette "safely entered the Mississippi . . . with a joy that I cannot express."

Above. A small tributary adds to the Mississippi near Marquette, Iowa.

Right. Upper Mississippi flood plain in spring

Above. Dubuque, Iowa

Right. The arrival of the *Delta Queen* draws spectators to the river's edge.

I N 1823 Captain John Crawford was making history ever so cautiously. His little blue sternwheeler, *Virginia,* was the first steamboat ever to know the uncharted channel of the upper Mississippi. Departing St. Louis, she survived the rocks of the Des Moines rapids, numerous groundings on sand bars, and narrowly escaped a forest fire on this historic first voyage to the Falls of St. Anthony.

Guns and powder, whiskey, merchants, pioneers, and tourists—these were some of the new cargoes brought by steamboats, betokening changing lifeways along the Mississippi River.

The artist George Catlin came up with the idea of a "Fashionable Tour . . . by steamer" a century and a half ago. It would be a journey through a splendid unspoiled region of picturesque bluffs and wooded islands, Indian villages and traders' shanties. The Fashionable Tour caught on. People came from Europe and the East Coast cities to see the American northwest frontier in relative comfort.

Passage could be booked between St. Louis and St. Paul with quite satisfactory accommodations for twelve dollars. On some of the boats the "fashionables" enjoyed entertainments provided by brass bands and dance orchestras, even the famous cornet of a Ned Kendall. The steam piano was a hit on Captain Ward's boat, the *Excelsior,* and served as matchless advertisement at the landings. Popular lectures, drinking, and gambling were other diversions. Some luxuriously appointed vessels were promoted as floating palaces. It was conspicuous consumption in a frontier setting, a peculiarly romantic and exciting novelty to urbanites.

The boats themselves provided sufficient reason for excitement: their average life expectancy was less than five years, what with collisions, boiler explosions, fires set off by sparks at the landings, and snags and submerged logs ready to destroy the hull of a paddlewheeler and sink the boat in fifteen minutes. Mark Twain's brother was killed in a steamboat explosion, and the worst accident ever on the Mississippi —the explosion of the *Sultana,* crammed with soldiers just released from Andersonville—took more lives than the sinking of the *Titanic.*

Dangers aside, steamboats were a vital part of the social life of innumerable towns on the Mississippi and her backwater streams. People were always at the landing to learn whatever the boat might be bringing of merchandise, news, or entertainment. Showboats such as French's *New Sensation* were special favorites, for they provided the immediacy of live theater in its broadest emotions.

Our interest in paddlewheelers today is a nostalgic visit to the river's past. Only one nineteenth-century passenger boat, the *Delta Queen,* vintage 1890, still plies the river between St. Louis and St. Paul in the grand style. Practically any convention-goer or sightseer on the river can take a short cruise on a paddleboat for a few dollars—and pretend for an hour.

At seven in the morning we reached Hannibal, Missouri, where my boyhood was spent. . . . I stepped ashore with the feeling of one who returns out of a dead-and-gone generation. . . . It is no longer a village; it is a city, . . . a thriving and energetic place, and is paved like the rest of the west and south. . . . A deal of money changes hands there now.

Mark Twain was astonished, even disillusioned over the changes he remarked in his boyhood town when he returned after an absence of several years. Hannibal may have been a disappointment, but the Mississippi did not let him down, for "it had suffered no change; it was as young and fresh and comely and gracious as ever it had been."

In *Old Glory,* a British writer and traveler, Jonathan Raban, looking to Hannibal for a timeless piece of Americana, found his own dream had been whitewashed. Others undoubtedly share his frustration:

Poor Huck. He had made horribly good. A hundred years later he was Hannibal's darling. The untamable boy . . . had turned into the pivot of that town's tourist industry. . . . Aunt Sally had won in the end, as Aunt Sally was bound to. Hannibal had adopted Twain's angry masterpiece and civilized it into a nice, profit-making chunk of sentimental kitsch.

We make an impatient tourist's mistake if we say, Is that all there is? Sometimes the significant reality for the traveler is not what we have come to look at, but what we have come to look for inside ourselves.

Above. Hannibal, Missouri

Left. ". . . how curiously the familiar and the strange were mixed together . . ."
—MARK TWAIN, *Life on the Mississippi,* 1883

Preceding pages. A towboat searches for buoys in the predawn. Can buoys mark one side of the channel, nun buoys the other.

This page. The Lone Eagle Ferry, last paddlewheel ferry on the Mississippi River

Left. Farm couple from Bowling Green, Missouri, selling apples in the midwestern heartland

Next two pages. Independence Day celebration, said to be the biggest in the country, in St. Louis, Missouri

61

ASSING beneath the Eads Bridge at St. Louis, we leave the upper Mississippi behind. The river widens now, fed by the waters of the Missouri River, and runs through a lazy succession of meandering loops; it is also more unpredictable now, despite an appearance of indolence. This is the beginning of the lower Mississippi, a river difficult to bridge because of her tendency to flood.

The man who conceived the graceful bridge spanning the Mississippi just a few yards from the Gateway Arch knew the river intimately. James Eads was already a young steamboat clerk when Mark Twain's family moved to Hannibal. By the age of twenty-two he had started a profitable business in underwater salvage, cleaning up the wreckage from steamboat accidents around St. Louis. He invented a diving bell for the purpose, and with it he observed the constantly changing character of the river bottom.

James Eads had never built a bridge; he wasn't even an engineer. Someone recognized his genius, however, for he got the contract that would make St. Louis a rail center. He successfully countered the resistance of the army engineers and the steamboat companies. He stood firm before the powerful interests of the Chicago railroads, who were out to crush any St. Louis competition.

He had many setbacks, but the bridge Eads built marked a visible transition from mundane to inspired engineering. It was the first entirely cantilevered construction made of steel, using longer spans than any bridge had ever incorporated before. Its curves hung suspended in air as gracefully as the crescent bends of the river lay over the land. To this day the double-decker Eads bridge remains in use, and it has required very little maintenance since it opened in 1874.

Left and above. Two views of Eads Bridge

Above. The proprietress of Bonnie's Bar on Bloody Island, East St. Louis. When the sandbar really was an island, unclaimed by either Missouri or Illinois, it was a popular site for duelists.

Right. Enjoying an afternoon of repose on the general store's outdoor bench, just south of Cape Girardeau, Missouri

MISSISSIPPI
Lower River

THE Mississippi is joined by the Ohio at Cairo, Illinois, halfway to the sea. It is an unwilling alliance, and their waters do not mingle easily. The heavy brown Mississippi hugs the Missouri shore, while the translucent Ohio keeps to the Kentucky bank. On a sunny day you can see a distinct line between the moving waters.

The Mississippi has just doubled in volume, for the Ohio contributes its huge drainage from the Northeast and the Appalachians. Below Cairo, the once-fresh Mississippi assumes a dirty, industrial, and dangerous aspect. The river towns are more commercially than residentially oriented; the water is no longer suited to small pleasure craft or fishing or swimming.

People are not as close to the river along its lower reaches. The upper river is dotted with small communities touching the riverbanks, but below Cairo there are many fewer towns, and they tend to be situated on high bluffs wherever possible. The seeking of high ground is a lower river habit, formed of necessity.

The lower Mississippi is uneasily restrained between man-made walls called lev-

ees. They are a perpetual reminder of the menace the river is deemed to present to human life and property. Ever since the War Department took over responsibility for the Mississippi River in 1824, it has promoted levee building, regarding its job with the river as one of doing battle with an implacable enemy. The levees, down both sides of the lower river, total nearly 1600 miles, longer than the Great Wall of China.

Levee repair and maintenance is a serious, longterm undertaking. The earthwork appears solid, but a creature as tiny as a fiddler crab can do terrific damage with its tunneling. One day a little water enters a pocket gopher's or a muskrat's or an armadillo's burrow . . . and the entire structure begins to dissolve from the inside. Gigantic concrete mattresses laid down on the river bottom and against the levees to buttress the earth must be replaced every few years.

In route and intent, the lower Mississippi is devious. There are so many long and lazy curves, so many bends and loops to negotiate, that the river distance between Cape Girardeau in Missouri and the Gulf is twice the actual distance. There are no

Above. The waters of the Ohio and Mississippi rivers meet, but they do not mingle for some miles.

Left. Reelfoot Lake, Tennessee, created by the 1811 earthquake

rapids here to shatter a hull, as there were in the upper river, but the water conceals other hazards. Because there are no dams on this stretch of the river to slow the current, millraces develop when the river cuts off over the narrow necks of land between bends. An unexpected switch in the main channel is characteristic of the lower river; the Mississippi is not necessarily the same stream from one day to the next.

It was a turbid Mississippi in the fullness of spring flood, a two-mile-wide onrush of uprooted trees and alluvial earth, when the first European saw the river in 1541. Hernando De Soto and his beleaguered army had been slogging through cypress swamps, herding their pigs before them and cursing mosquitoes for nearly two years, hoping to find the gold of another Peru. There was no gold, only the biggest river his chroniclers had ever seen. They named it Rio Grande.

Foreigners ever since have been impressed by the Mississippi's size and the profusion of lush landscape in these lower reaches, but the early travelers also feared its sudden dangers—the boils in the water that could suck them under, the plague that might take them in the hot summer.

The lower Mississippi was the stretch that Americans came to know first. "Old Man River" many call it, a personification of something vital and enduring, an image deriving from some ultimately optimistic place in our national imagination.

As a people we drank a bitter cup here during the Civil War. Perhaps it is the poignancy of human innocence and tragedy we most see reflected in the lower river.

Left. The lower Mississippi often changes its channel. The once-thriving metropolis of Napoleon, Arkansas, now lies completely beneath the water.

Preceding pages. Diesel towboats on the lower river, where there are no locks and dams, may push fifty or sixty barges.

Above. "[Cairo, Illinois, was] the town that sent Ulysses S. Grant on from obscurity to failure and renown."

—J. R. HUMPHREYS, *The Last of the Middle West,* 1966

Right. People used to come from distant dry miles around to drink at the Turf Club in Cairo, Illinois.

HEY pronounce it *kay-row,* Illinois, and it is the zero point for all mileages up and down the Mississippi. Huddled at the confluence of the Ohio with the Mississippi, Cairo is protected by levees from her two rivers. It is a place accustomed to water; this was the original delta millions of years ago when a tropical sea came this far inland.

Land companies needed three tries to get the town started, but everyone thought it was bound to become the crossroads of commerce in America. The popular nickname for this rich corn country in southern Illinois was "Little Egypt." John Banvard's 1849 panorama touted Cairo as "destined to become one of the largest inland cities in the United States." Cairo almost met that destiny, for it was an important commercial center even before the North became industrialized. It was both a railhead and a major river port, with nearly 4,000 steamboats docking there even two years after the Civil War.

But the Civil War changed Cairo forever. Her citizens had wanted southern Illinois to leave the Union and form a separate state. Her seemingly favorable geographic location became a strain, not only economically and politically, but psychically for her people. Cairo was at heart a southern town, with all the benefits and all the burdens that entailed.

Today, traveling from the North to Cairo, you know you have crossed into the South. Tupelo and cypress grow out of the water at Horseshoe Lake, but the faintly tropical scent of magnolia and the mild touch of the breeze here cannot hide a perceptible tension in the air. The town has never been able to leave behind completely the racial and economic problems tearing at her social fabric.

People drift away, their houses stand in neglect and disrepair. Kudzu vine overgrowing the railyard on the river gives the impression that Cairo's time of glory is past.

Above and right. A river man on the Kentucky side of the Mississippi displays his distaste for unwanted strangers.

THERE are places on the river where you get a sense of "bad water," a feeling that anything might happen. In 1673, Father Marquette was warned by some Great Lakes Indians about "horrible monsters, which devoured men and canoes together."

Some three hundred years later, Jonathan Raban found himself on the same section of river. He describes a place near Tomato, Arkansas, on a stretch of mile-wide water that was deceptively easy:

> I couldn't work out what was wrong. I seemed to be going faster than I'd ever been before, with the entire surface of the river pouring by in a glassy race of logs, twigs, cola cans and orange crates. . . . I had quite lost my sense of place and dimension.

What is remarkable about all this is—nothing. This is the Mississippi, a river to be closely watched, always. Raban continues, recalling "a queer, scary elation in feeling myself poised so fragilely on that sweep of water, watching the forest and sky tremble and start to run. I had touched the deep stillness of the Mississippi; it was as if the world moved around the river and not the river through the world."

Strange things have always been happening on the river. The year 1811 did not augur well for Mississippi country. The biggest spring flood in a quarter-century left pestilence over the land. A summer "cold plague" stunted the crops, then hailstones beat them into the earth. Millions of gray squirrels, like so many lemmings, tried to swim across the river; passenger pigeons roosted in flocks so tremendous they broke the trees. A solar eclipse revealed a comet, which many people interpreted as a disaster warning.

Finally, the night of December 16, 1811, what was probably the strongest earthquake ever to sunder the United States had its epicenter on the river, at New Madrid, Missouri, a small town a few miles downriver from Cairo. Aftershocks continued for two months. That was the night the Mississippi River ran upstream, the night the northwestern corner of Tennessee dropped nearly twenty feet, and Reelfoot Lake was created in an instant. The lake is still there, on top of a bald cypress forest.

The notion of "bad water" is certainly reinforced along the lower Mississippi by the presence of the levees, because the threat of disaster is their very reason for being. But there is something else, too, especially if you are a stranger here. You feel vulnerable, as though exposed to unknown, unreasonable risks should you venture off the main channel. There is sightseeing, and then there is trespassing, and you want to keep them straight.

You step into a time warp here, in some places along the Mississippi, into a rural isolation so profound that your ordinary rules of behavior, your expectations of order, do not apply. In such a place, you understand that the river, and the folk dwelling there, take you on their terms.

Left. Memphis, Tennessee. Old Man River is a mirror to something constant, something enduring in the human spirit. You can hear it sung in the blues—the pain and the humor, both—on the golden haze of a Memphis evening. For it was here the blues were conceived, and "Memphis Blues" was the firstborn. This original black American folk music spills over with the emotions of the life lived and worked out here, along the Mississippi.

Some titles suggest the river's changeable presence:

"Traveling Riverside Blues"
"Southern High Water"
"Risin' High Water Blues"
"Sleepy Water Blues"
"Mississippi Heavy Water Blues"

Others tell of the age-old troubles:

"Honey Dripper Blues"
"All Around Mama"
"Ask My Sister, Please Don't Be Like Me"
"A Woman Gets Tired of the Same Man All the Time"
"Worried Life Blues"
"Somewhere, Before Long"
"I'd Rather Drink Muddy Water"

But relief is at hand:

"Cool Drink of Water Blues"
"Cooling Board"
"From Four Until Late"
"Goin' Back to Memphis"

Preceding pages. Andrew Jackson foresaw greatness for the town he platted and named Memphis, Tennessee.

Right. The blues gave voice to some of America's most expressive musicians: Muddy Waters; Mississippi John Hurt; Memphis Minnie; Memphis Slim; Jimmie Rodgers; Howling Wolf; Ma Rainey; Robert Johnson; Bukka White; Furry Lewis; Mance Lipscom; Brownie McGhee; T-Bone Walker; Leadbelly; Lightnin' Hopkins; Big Bill Broonzy; John Lee Hooker; Joe Williams; Son House; Jimmie and Walter.

Left. A third of the American cotton crop passes through the Memphis Cotton Exchange every year, and the city is the largest spot cotton market in the world. Several of the old cotton warehouses you see on Front Street today have been saved for another glory—the tourist trade.

Below. Changing of the guard at the Peabody Hotel, Memphis

COTTON, Beale Street, and the new Peabody—you could hardly miss these hallmarks of the Memphis scene on the Mississippi River.

The cobblestones paving the steeply sloping Memphis waterfront arrived as ballast on Dutch ships. Over the last century the stones have been worn smooth by the laboring steps of men and mules in the service of King Cotton. Countless buyers have called at this port with a nearly insatiable appetite for the white fiber billowing out over the fertile bottomlands around Memphis.

There was always music to be heard on the waterfront and in the fields. W. C. Handy listened, and when he put that first composition to paper in 1912, he called it "Memphis Blues." The blues grew out of black life in the white South. A genuine folk music, the blues is a feeling, a poignancy, a plaintiveness, a bawdy humor, a music for survivors. The blues was christened in Beale Street, the black commercial district of Memphis, a neighborhood of saloons and bordellos, pawnshops, pool halls, and the First Baptist Church, Beale.

Urban renewal had much of Beale Street bulldozed in the sixties, but now another phase of redevelopment is underway. Renovation of historical districts is aimed at attracting investors and visitors with money to spend in trendy shops and restaurants.

Left. "The military engineers . . . are building wing dams here and there, to deflect the current; and dikes to confine it in narrower bounds . . . and for unnumbered miles along the Mississippi, they are felling the timberfront . . . and in many places they have protected the wasting shores with rows of piles. One who knows the Mississippi will promptly aver . . . that ten thousand River Commissions . . . cannot tame that lawless stream . . . cannot say to it, Go here, or Go there, and make it obey; cannot save a shore which it has sentenced; cannot bar its path with an obstruction which it will not tear down, dance over, and laugh at."
—MARK TWAIN, *Life on the Mississippi,* 1883

Right. Every year the Mississippi rises with spring meltwaters and summer rains accumulated from nearly half the United States. The lower river runs wide, meandering where it wills, banked by levees. As William Faulkner told it, when the levee above Greenville, Mississippi, broke in 1927, no one knew "whether the river had become lost in a drowned world or if the world had become drowned in one limitless river." Filthy water and swirling trees and dead animals and household belongings were strewn out over 26,000 square miles of the lower Mississippi valley. That year 200,000 people drowned; over half a million lost their homes.

IVER BARGES, each weighing well over three hundred tons, are strung together into tows. A diesel-powered barge tow on the lower river may incorporate fifty or even sixty such barges. A tiny human pilot sits at his panel of steering levers in the multidecked towboat behind this 1200-foot-long, five-acre steel platform and exercises a remarkable degree of directional control over the entire moving island. Even with 4000 horsepower, though, a barge tow will need a quarter of a mile to stop, and the wash created by its passage makes it dangerous to be near in a small craft.

Seeing such a thing coming downstream can be humbling.

Seeing one from above, all its units in close-packed order, the barge tow is a thing of precise geometric harmony. The massiveness, the density of the individual parts, makes the whole the more amazing: dozens of barges lashed together with steel cables and propelled by a single towboat that pushes, rather than pulls, the bulky platform through the water.

Greenville, Mississippi, makes those marvelous towboats. She has done well for herself as a towboat city, despite the fact that the fickle Mississippi one day made a new channel and left the riverport behind on an abandoned loop. Engineers constructed a passage to reconnect the town to the river, and now Greenville is a slackwater port with a barge-building yard and marine repair shops.

This inland port has a customs office to handle shipments abroad; miniships make it a seaport over five hundred miles upriver from the Gulf, and the new container and hoisting technologies have stimulated barge traffic.

Above. Using the buddy system, a tow pilot has a guide to steer down the deepest part of the channel.

Right. Greenville, Mississippi, longtime "Towboat Capital of the World"

86

Above. The South has a long memory. Northerners speak of the Civil War, southerners call it "the War."

Above. When Vicksburg fell to Grant's forces after a forty-seven-day siege, the Mississippi River became a Union stream.

T HE Atchafalaya River is the Mississippi's major distributary, and its union with the big river near Simmesport, Louisiana, sixty miles upstream of Baton Rouge, is through Old River. At this narrow and vulnerable juncture is a major flood control dam: the Old River Control Structure. The prosaic name belies an incredible purpose.

The government's plan is to keep the Mississippi River from doing again what it has already done several times in the last few thousand years—keep it from making a new main channel, forming a new delta. The river's present course takes it conveniently past Baton Rouge and New Orleans. What the river wants to do is bypass those cities altogether and cut directly south toward Morgan City and the Gulf via the Atchafalaya, saving nearly two hundred miles.

In the early 1940s it was predicted that the Mississippi was going to alter its course by 1975 if no one did anything. The prediction was never tested, because the army engineers started levee building, and in 1963 they added the control structure to regulate the amount of Mississippi water escaping through the Atchafalaya.

The Atchafalaya carries off about a third of the Mississippi's total volume of water. As it rushes down the Atchafalaya channel, cutting it ever deeper, more silt is carried to the new delta, just south of Morgan City.

The engineers try to plan for once-a-century superfloods. Although the big flood of 1973 was not of that category, it severely damaged the Old River Control Sructure. Those who live in the delta are betting the river will finish the job, sooner if not later.

Right. The Old River Control Structure, near Simmesport, Louisiana

WO fantasy buildings are visible from the river at Baton Rouge. The new statehouse, the country's tallest skyscraper capitol, was built during "Kingfish" Huey Long's administration as part of his Depression Era public works projects. This was the same Huey Long who built a low bridge over the Mississippi to discourage river traffic and money from going on past Baton Rouge.

The other fantasy building looks just like a medieval castle. Mark Twain held Sir Walter Scott responsible for the old statehouse,

> for it is not conceivable that this little sham castle would ever have been built if he had not run the people mad . . . with his medieval romances. . . . It is pathetic enough that a whitewashed castle, with turrets and things . . . should ever have been built in

this otherwise honorable place; but it is much more pathetic to see this architectural falsehood undergoing restoration and perpetuation in our day, when it would have been so easy to let dynamite finish what a charitable fire began, and then devote this restoration money to the building of something genuine.

At least the park surrounding the old capitol met with Twain's approval and it remains much the same today. He saw Baton Rouge "clothed in flowers, like a bride. . . . The magnolia trees in the Capitol grounds were lovely and fragrant, with their dense rich foliage and huge snowball blossoms. The scent of the flower is very sweet, but you want distance on it, because it is so powerful."

A tropical southern dreaminess in only one feature of the modern Baton Rouge. That aspect of the city's history seems hardly to have been possible when we see what Baton Rouge now is to the industrial world.

Above. Old State Capitol at Baton Rouge

Left. Exxon Plant at Baton Rouge

TO the river traveler who has just floated through miles of a luscious monotony of forestland set aside in wildlife management areas, the sight of contemporary Baton Rouge must come as a shock.

A recent visitor was dismayed by his impression of a city that "had leaked, in a diluted form, down miles and miles of river, spreading its oil and chemical plants along the levees, turning the landscape into an unlovable abstraction of wire, aluminum and tarmac."

Baton Rouge is a gigantic petrochemical complex. The city is a labyrinth of pipes and oil storage tanks, and the 2000-acre Exxon oil refinery lying against the river on the north edge of town is the country's largest. Hundreds of thousands of barrels of crude from fields in Texas, Louisiana, and Mississippi are processed in Baton Rouge every day. Hundreds of oil-based products, the stuff of our daily lives, are shipped out in tankers and barges from this deep-water ocean port to markets all over the world. Gasoline, jet fuel, kerosene, greases and waxes, naptha, asphalt—it all rides the Mississippi.

Industry has claimed several thousand acres of prime riverside agricultural land in recent years, land that used to be devoted to sugarcane. The Jesuits introduced sugarcane here in 1751, and both cane and rice flourish in these lowlands. The so-called "sugar coast" extends between Baton Rouge and the mouth of the Mississippi, the same area where oil is so important.

Two views of Baton Rouge, Louisiana: petrochemicals *(left)* and sugarcane *(above)*

FLOURISHING, if ultimately distressing, underpinning of the lower Mississippi River's economy was the plantation. Mark Twain recalled the scene from the early nineteenth century:

From Baton Rouge to New Orleans, the great sugar plantations border both sides of the river all the way, and stretch their league-wide levels back to the dim forest walls of bearded cypress in the rear. . . . Plenty of dwellings all the way, on both banks—standing so close together, for long distances, that the broad river lying between the two rows, becomes a sort of spacious street. . . . And now and then you see a pillared and porticoed great manorhouse, embowered in trees. Here is testimony of one or two of the procession of foreign tourists that filed along here half a century ago. Mrs. Trollope says:—

The unbroken flatness of the banks of the Mississippi continued unvaried for many miles above New Orleans; but the graceful and luxuriant palmetto, the dark and noble ilex, and the bright orange, were everywhere to be seen, and it was many days before we were weary of looking at them.

Captain Basil Hall:—

The district of country which lies adjacent to the Mississippi, in the lower parts of Louisiana, is everywhere thickly peopled by sugar planters, whose showy houses, gay piazzas, trig gardens, and numerous slave villages, all clean and neat, gave an exceedingly thriving air to the river scenery.

Preceding pages. Oceangoing vessel wending its way to the Gulf from Baton Rouge. The channel here is seventy feet deep.

Above. Springtime blossoms

Left. Nottoway, the largest plantation home on the Mississippi River

Above. Live oaks at Oak Alley, Louisiana

Above. A traditional Christmas bonfire on the levee

NEW ORLEANS is justifiably the most famous town on the Mississippi River. It is a stimulating city, delighting in its differences. No homogenous melting pot, this New Orleans, but a spicy mix of tastes and sights and sounds to celebrate diverse heritage. For gourmets, the city offers endless delights: Creole gumbo; crawfish bisque and Jambalay shrimp; beignets and café au lait; licorice root, Paul Prudhomme, and dinner at Antoine's. For music lovers, the streets called Bourbon and Basin are vibrant with Dixieland jazz and the music of Louis Armstrong, Dr. John, and Jelly Roll Morton. For tourists there is the French Quarter, Storyville, the above-ground cemeteries, Congo Square, Lake Pontchartrain, and, of course, Mardi Gras. Her citizens come from the world at large; her history, replete with pirates, plantations, and politicians, is various and lively.

Above. New Orleans

Right. Mardi Gras, the celebration that sets the standard for fun and festivity

Above. Musician ponders the river and cargo ships, New Orleans.

Preceding pages. Cargo ship at anchor, New Orleans

Above. Dejan's Olympia Brass Band of New Orleans

Above and below. French Quarter. New Orleans is a colorful gumbo of many old worlds.

Right. Detail of graceful ornamental grillwork. The Lafitte brothers used their blacksmith shop in New Orleans as a cover for piracy.

New Orleans in 1823 must have been an exquisite torment to a man as concerned with his physical health as Timothy Flint was. The city captured his cosmopolitan imagination, but for "one dreary drawback—the insalubrity of its situation." Swamps and yellow fever were a constant worry to Reverend Flint. Epidemics carried off thousands of victims, permitting him ample opportunity to contemplate the disposition of the body.

> Of course, the graves that are dug . . . will have one or two feet of water. One of the circumstances dreadful to the imagination of a sick stranger, is the probability of being buried in the water. To prevent this, all . . . whose estates are sufficient, have their remains deposited in tombs or vaults above ground.

These cities of the dead are still among the most well-known attractions of New Orleans, a city that receives nearly sixty inches of rain annually. The city's twenty-four-hour-a-day pumping stations discharge fifty to sixty million gallons of excess water daily into the canals leading to Lake Pontchartrain. Pumping Station No. 6, the world's largest, can handle 6,450 cubic feet of water per second. Life in the shadow of the levees continues as usual, as long as the river runs along neatly inside, five feet above street level on a dry day, eighteen or more feet during high-water periods.

Above. New Orleans used water wheels in the past, but twenty-one pumping stations keep the city dry now.

Right. A city of the dead in New Orleans

"This city exhibits the greatest variety of costume. . . . There is a sample, in short, of everything."
—TIMOTHY FLINT, *Recollections of the Last Ten Years,* 1826

Following pages. With only a few miles between it and the ocean, a freighter heads down South Pass to the end of the Mississippi River.

MISSISSIPPI
Delta

THE Mississippi Delta is land both created and shaped by its river. Ambiguous union of fluid and firm, the delta is a liquid land where life responds to both tidal and freshwater urgings. The processes of creation have been going on for a long time here, just as they have at the headwaters. For this is where the cycle begins again, the river entering the sea.

Approaching the end of the Mississippi River, it seems we are come to its beginning again. The river was conceived in bogs, and it fulfills its birthright through delta marshlands. Myriad headwater streams converged like limbs of a willow at the main stem of the river. Now the delta mirrors that branching image, the river's numerous distributary courses reaching out to the sea.

Like the headwaters, there is about the delta something original, primeval. We look to the delta for many of the oldest continuing life forms: alligators, holdovers from the gigantic lizards of the dinosaur age; wizened, black-garbed cormorants hunching on cypress stumps between dives for fish; thousand-year-old bald cypress trees, the longest-lived beings in the Mississippi Valley, and more closely related to sequoias than to other contemporaries.

Many of the birds here have borrowed characteristics from an earlier perch along the tree of life: the reptilian neck and hairlike feathers of snakebirds; the gaunt and ponderous wings of great blue herons; the harsh croaking voices of roseate spoonbills; the wrinkled folds of the brown pelican's pouch.

Left. Delta alligator

Mallards, teals, and pintails; sandpipers, plovers, avocets; various herons, ibises, egrets—an incredible diversity of ducks, shorebirds, and waders thrives in this river delta wilderness, a land that is always flowing, cleansing, and remaking itself.

The delta is a lacework of bayous. The word comes from *bayuk,* Choctaw for "creek." Like the river, the bayous may dry up, change channels, or disappear from one location to reappear in another, depending on variations in the water table. Water may flow in both directions, following the Gulf tides.

Bayou country has always belonged to individualists, just as the headwaters region attracts only a sparse population of independent souls. Cajuns have been self-sufficiently doing things their own way since 1755, when the first Acadians found refuge in the delta.

The dark cypress swamp bayous of popular imagination—the ones draped in Spanish moss—do exist. Such a bayou landscape figures prominently in Faulkner's version of the deluge story, *The Wild Palms.* There you would find yourself "slogging and stumbling knee-deep in something less of earth than water, along one of those black winding channels less of water than earth."

The present delta is composed of topsoils from two thousand miles upstream.

Above. "In the Delta, most of the world seemed sky. . . . The land was perfectly flat and level but it shimmered like the wing of a lighted dragonfly. It seemed strummed, as though it were an instrument and something had touched it."

—EUDORA WELTY, *Delta Wedding,* 1945

There is so much sediment that the water, twisting and squeezing its way into devious exits, is literally being forced to seek a new, more straightforward route to the sea. The Mississippi has chosen her new channel already: the Atchafalaya River.

Six times since the end of the last ice age the Mississippi has changed course at its delta, abandoning the old to adopt a new one. Human intervention in recent centuries has only delayed the natural order of events. New Orleanians are justifiably concerned by the possibility of losing their river's embrace, yet the Crescent City has existed for hardly a moment by the river's clock.

In this watery region, the Mississippi moves deliberately, an irrepressible tide of waters gathered from across the continent, committed to finish what has been a very long journey.

Left. Stalking frogs among the cypress knees

Right. Bayou Petit Caillou, or "little pebble"

Left. A Cajun repairs his net.

Preceding pages. A sunrise congress of delta birds: ibis, spoonbill, great egret, heron

TO imagine the delta's future we think of both permanence and change.

The notion of permanence can be altogether different here. Live oak trees, for example, solid citizens of the forest, will survive just a few yards from the water's margin, on a slight rise of land. With the growing Atchafalaya delta, there is another phenomenon of oaks. *Cheniers* are ridges of silt, mud, and shells paralleling the western Louisiana Gulf coastline, several miles out at sea. Live oaks flourish on them, their own roots helping to hold the soil together. Nevertheless, these trees are not immune to the forces of violent destruction. Severe winds and waves can take oak as easily as willow.

Permanence assumes still another dimension in the delicate lavender petals of the water hyacinth. These decorative plants entered the United States during the 1884 New Orleans Cotton Exhibition. It wasn't long before water hyacinths were literally choking out the big delta bullfrogs, muskrats, fish, and ducks, as well as all other plants living in the local swamps and bayous. Worse, each year's dormant hyacinth seeds may remain viable for twenty years.

The delta is home to reptiles and fish as old as alligators and gars, to trees like the cypress that live submerged in water, their gnarled "knees" rising to the air. It is refuge to migrant birds from the north, like the loon, which can adapt to both fresh and salt water. Ancient forms, one and all, but they are the more tenuous because of our own presence here. On just one day in 1821 John Audubon recorded a deliberate sport kill of over 48,000 plovers at one site along the river. Snowy egrets were at risk until the plume fashion in ladies' hats went out of style in Europe. The brown pelican, Louisiana's state bird, was decimated in the sixties by runoff from cotton pesticides. A breeding population had to be imported from Florida.

Other wild lives are found from the headwaters to the delta, the river being the very life thread of the wilderness fabric. Parula warblers nest in lichens in the north, and in Spanish moss in the south. The fragrant partridge berry, a ground cover among northern white pine needles, is also discovered at local spots along the river, and among the long-leafed pine woods of the south. Other small beauties: groundsel, wild iris, and the jewelweed that grows at Lake Itasca and in Louisiana.

The Mississippi River begins and ends in places of sanctuary for wild creatures. Civilization, though, is much closer here than it is in the headwaters. Dense clusters of huge offshore oil wells surround the delta. One-eighth of the country's oil comes from the same waters that provide 40 percent of our commercial fish catch. The threat of oil spills is always present, but degradation of the land by the canals is actual. These canals, built for equipment access and for the laying of pipelines, hasten both erosion and saltwater intrusion into the delta's freshwater areas.

A century ago the main pass out to the sea was too silted to permit even flat-bottomed steamers to make it through the shallow water. Captain Eads devised parallel jetties to force the river to scour its own main channel, taking the sediment straight out to the Gulf. Today ships of ocean draft can use the channel.

The drawback to the jetties has been the loss of the rich river deposit. The delta now is built up right to the edge of the continental shelf, so the channel silt sinks uselessly into the depths of the abyss. It is no longer available to create new delta land, as it had been doing for thousands of years, ever since Cairo was a coastal region. The present Mississippi delta and the eastern coast of Louisiana are losing about fifty square miles of marshland annually because the levees and jetties prevent the river sediments from entering and enriching those fragile coastal marshes.

Above. Saltwater marsh near Houma, Louisiana

Right. Great egret

Even as the Mississippi River's own delta loses land to the sea, the western Gulf coastal area, especially the mouth of the Atchafalaya, resting in a shallow bay, is gaining dozens of new islands. The islands are V-shaped, pointing upstream, and each new flood enlarges the original islands, adds new ones, and promotes conditions for the arrival of plant life. Marsh arrowheads are the earliest plant colonizers, soon followed by willows. The willow is found the entire length of the Mississippi River, and it has remained essentially unchanged for 130 million years.

Ultimate capture of all the Mississippi waters by the Atchafalaya River seems inevitable. While the great river is reluctant to remain in her old bed, she will be in charge of the delta as long as she does stay there. Charles Latrobe recognized the same evidence of the river's dominion in 1843 when he was returning to Europe:

> Long after we had lost sight of the land, the turbid waters heaving around us told us we were still in the domain and influence of the Mississippi. At length we shot over a line clearly defined and distinct—passed from a yellow wave into one of sea-green hue —and bade adieu to the mighty Father of Waters.

Above. A delta towboat heads west on the Intracoastal Waterway near Houma, Louisiana. This distributary, the Atchafalaya River, will become the future Mississippi.

Left. Pulling an offshore oil rig out to its home in the Gulf just beyond the passes

Next page. Born in wilderness bogs, the Mississippi River returns to the sea through marshlands.